Mount Hope Cemetery

# By-laws of the Trustees of Mount Hope Cementery

of the city of Boston, with a list of the proprietors, avenues, walks, paths

Mount Hope Cemetery

**By-laws of the Trustees of Mount Hope Cementery**
*of the city of Boston, with a list of the proprietors, avenues, walks, paths*

ISBN/EAN: 9783337101763

Printed in Europe, USA, Canada, Australia, Japan

Cover: Foto ©ninafisch / pixelio.de

More available books at **www.hansebooks.com**

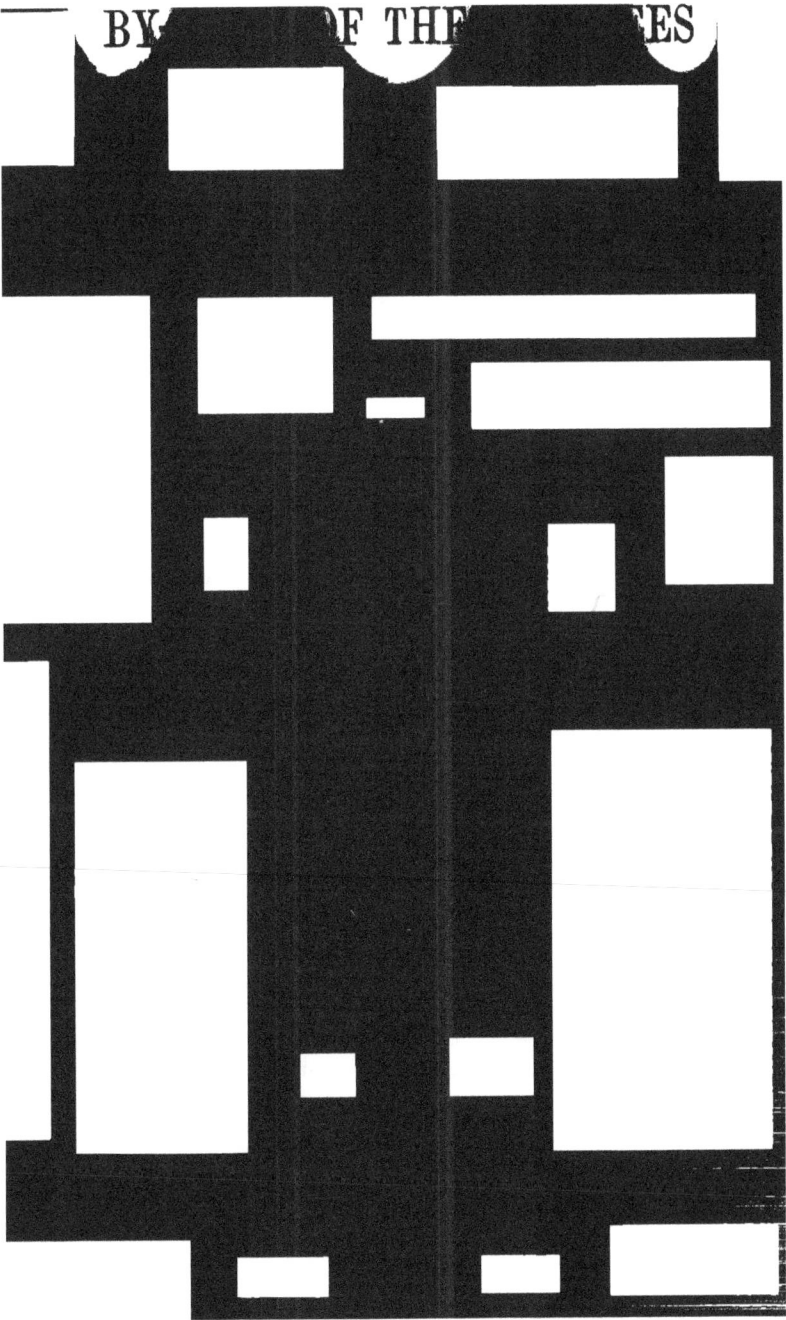

Mount Hope Cemetery is situated in the Dorchester District about 5 1-2 miles from the City Hall. It originally contained eighty-four and three-fourths acres, and was set apart for a Cemetery by individuals who were incorporated under powers given by the Revised Statutes, November 10, 1851, and was consecrated by appropriate ceremonies June 24, 1852. Sales of four hundred and twenty-seven lots were made by the Company and improvements were in progress from year to year. By deed, dated July 31, 1857, it was conveyed to the city for the sum of $35,000. In 1868 the city purchased an additional lot of twenty acres, on the northerly side, for $14,000, so that the Cemetery comprises at the present time an area of over one hundred and four acres. The proceeds of sales of lots are paid into the City Treasury, kept separate from other funds of the city; and, under the direction of the Trustees, expended in improvements of the Cemetery.

From the first of May to the first of November the present year, conveyance to the Cemetery can be had by the cars of the Boston and Providence Railroad, which leave Boston at 10.10, 11.30 A. M., and 2.40 P. M., and by the cars of the Old Colony and Newport Railroad, which leave Boston for Mattapan at 1 P. M., and by the Forest Hills horse cars, which leave Boston at 11 A. M., 2 and 3 P. M. Returning, the Cemetery coach will connect with the steam cars of the Providence Road for Boston at 11 A. M., 2.15, 3.53 and 5.19 P. M., and the horse cars from Forest Hills at 11 A. M., 4 and 5.30 P. M., and the steam cars of the Hartford and Erie Road at 1.08 P. M., and the Old Colony Road at 4.40 P. M.

Besides the natural beauty of the grounds, and the art which has improved and embellished them, there are several objects of interest to invite visits from citizens and strangers to the Cemetery. Its location is in one of the most attractive valleys of Eastern Massachusetts, and the landscape view secured by its highest elevation can hardly be surpassed in the vicinity. The floral display at the proper season has been pronounced by competent authority unequalled by that of any Cemetery in the neighborhood of Boston. The Army and Navy Monument, erected to commemorate the heroic dead of Boston in the great struggle for nationality, is regarded as one of the most chaste and successful of the many similar structures that have been erected. The Odd Fellows' Memorial, about to be erected, and a beautiful artificial lake now in process of construction, will soon add their attractions;

# MANA

By the Ordina
Cemetery is veste
elected annually,
from the citizens
two members of t
removal from offi
President from it
business.

The Board has
Cemetery.

The Board is a
of property, upon
improvement or
pair, preservation
for the planting o
lot, or for improv
sistent with the p
to the terms of su

The Board of T
lots to the impo
same. For the su
be given for the
hundred square
sufficient to provi

The annual car
perintendent, the
of labor required

# BY-LAWS OF THE TRUSTEES.

annual meetin
he first Monday
e chosen a Pres
ensuing year.
ent shall nomina
mmittee on Gro
mittee on Intern
Board shall co
ll call a spec
two Trustees.
ngs of the Tr
, and on the
t when the 22
en the meetin
d

### PRESIDENT.

**Art. 2.** The President shall preside at the meeting of the Trustees. He shall determine the hour and place for the meetings. He shall, unless otherwise ordered, nominate all committees; he shall sign the deeds of conveyance of lots, and bonds given for the perpetual care of the same; he shall make the annual and other Reports to the City Council, and perform such other duties as are required by the ordinances o the city. All bills on account of the Cemetery shall be approved by him before they are presented to the city for payment. In the absence of the President his duties shall be performed by the se present.

## SUPERINTENDENT.

ART. 4. The Superintendent shall resi    he Cemetery, and, under the direction of the Trustees, shall have the general supervision and custody thereof; shall keep the avenues, paths and grounds in neat and satisfactory order; and, as agent for the Trustees, shall have the sole power to engage and discharge workmen; also to order and ar ange their respective duties, and to pay their wages at such times and in uch manner as the Trustees shall direct. He shall ee that all regulations with regard to interments and he construction of tombs, monuments and fences, are complied with. He shall see that the rights of the city and regulations of the Trustees are respected by artists, mechanics and laborers employed on the grounds by individual proprietors. He shall fulfil all contracts made with proprietors for the repair of lots, or for their permanent care, and perform such other duties as the Trustees may require. He shall have power to remove from the Cemetery improper and disorderly persons, to abate nuisances, and to remove rubbish and unnecessary incumbrances. He shall keep, in books provided for the purpose, regular and accurate records of all interments, including the names and ages of the persons interred, and the place and date of their interment; also, of all monuments erected, and lots enclosed and improved. Also, of all moneys received or disbursed by him, whether for wages, fees, improvement of lots, sales of any kind, purchases made, or services rendered. On the first day of each month, or oftener, if required by the Trustees, he shall render to the Secretary copies of said accounts, with proper vouchers, and pay over to him all moneys remaining in his hands. He shall also render to the Secretary on the first day of each month a statement showing the number of interments made for the preceding month. The compensation of the Superintendent shall be a salary, to be fixed by the Trustees, and the use of the dwelling-house connected with the Cem-

etery, and no other perquisites; and he
remov

**COMMITTEE ON LOTS**

ART. 7. The Committee on Lots shall
three Trustees. They shall have the general supervision of all sales, locations and enlargements of lots;

No interment shall be made at Mount Hope such a permit as may be required by the laws of the State, or of the city or town from which the deceased may be brought, together with an order from the proprietor of the lot in which the interment is to be made, or from his legal representative, shall be presented to the Superintendent; *nor until the fees have been paid.*

No removal of bodies from the Cemetery will be permitted, except as provided by the laws of the State and in the manner prescribed by the Board of Health or orders of the Board of Trustees.

For an interment in a tomb a charge shall be made by the Superintendent according to the amount of service rendered in the case.

Until otherwise ordered, the fees for di████████ve and making an interment shall be : —

For a person 10 years of age and over█████████
   "        "    under 10 years,  . .
Each additional body interred in a g█
   same time, 10 years of age and ov█
Under 10 years, . . . . . . . █
D█posit in Receiving Tomb (see By-█
█, . . . . . . . . . . . █

### INTERMENTS IN CITY CE█

█10 years of age and over,
█nder 10 years, . . .

### LOTS AND SPACES.

█████ts shall be laid out by █
ent, █████████he approval of the Co█
In fu██████of lots, a space of no█
more ████████feet in width, at the█
Comm██████ts, shall be reserved█
limits o██████ lots, which space█
kept op████████thin which ther█
ments.

ART. 11. No slab or fence shall be erected upon or around any grave in Cypress Vale, or Maple Grove, without the approval of the Committee on Lots; and, as far as practicable, all memorial stones shall be of uniform size, conformable to a sample furnished by the Committee on Lots.

### SALES AND CONVEYANCES.

ART. 12. Lots applied for by purchasers may be laid out and graded by the Superintendent, subject to the approval of the Committee on Lots. If the sale is approved by the Committee, the purchaser shall then pay to the Secretary the customary, or stipulated price of the lot sold him, and shall receive a certificate therefor, which shall be returned to the Secretary when the deed is delivered. No deed of any lot shall be issued to more than one grantee, nor to any person as trustee, executor, or administrator, except by vote of the Trustees.

### TREES.

ART. 13. Trees standing within lots can be removed, if desired, by an application by the proprietor to the Superintendent, subject to the approval of the Committee on Grounds. The Committee on Grounds have also charge of the general subject of introducing and cultivating, trimming and removing trees and shrubs in other parts of the Cemetery.

## TOMBS.

ART. 14. Lots for tombs may be sold in places approved by the Trustees, and at prices fixed by them. Such tombs shall be constructed in a strong, tight and durable manner, and shall be in every part to the satisfaction of the Committee on Lots.

## RECEIVING TOMBS.

ART. 15. Bodies may be deposited in the receiving tomb, on payment of Ten Dollars to the Superintendent. If, within four months after such deposit, the body shall be interred in another part of the Cemetery by the friends of the deceased, no further charge shall be made for such interment; but if the body shall not be removed from the tomb within the period above specified, the Superintendent may cause the body to be interred in such place as shall be designated by the Committee on Interments. But if the friends desire further delay, the Superintendent, under the direction of the Committee on Interments, may allow the body to remain a longer time (not exceeding four months), on the payment of One Dollar per month in advance.

## MONUMENTS, STONES, FENCES, ETC.

ART 16. Proprietors have a right to erect on their lots, fences, monuments and ‘stones of appropriate character. Fences, tablets, or other devices of wood are not permitted. Evergreen hedges, of small or moderate size, are allowed.

ART. 17. No grave or tomb shall be opened for an interment or removal by any person except by order of the Trustees or Superintendent.

## FUNERALS.

ART. 18. Early notice of funerals should be given to the Superintendent at the Cemetery, who will make all the arrangements for the interment.

## OMNIBUSES, TEAMS, CARTS, ETC.

ART. 19. No teams or carts (except those used on the grounds) or omnibuses will be allowed to drive into the Cemetery without a special vote of the Trustees.

## ALTERATION OF BY-LAWS.

ART. 20. No addition to or alteration in the By-Laws shall be made at the same meeting at which it is proposed, nor unless adopted by a vote of the majority of the Trustees.

# RULES AND REGULATIONS TO BE OB-SERVED IN THE CEMETERY.

1. The Superintendent will receive visitors at all seasonable hours.

2. No person in the employ of the Superintendent is allowed to receive money for services rendered to visitors.

3. No horse is to be driven within the Cemetery faster than a walk, and no horses can be left in the grounds without a keeper, unless fastened to posts provided for the purpose.

4. All persons with fire-arms, or REFRESHMENTS, are prohibited from entering upon any part of the Cemetery grounds.

5. All persons are prohibited from writing upon, or otherwise defacing, any sign, monument, fence or other structure.

6. All persons are prohibited from gathering flowers, cutting or breaking any tree, plant or shrub.

7. Visitors will not be permitted to walk on the flower-beds, or upon the graded lots or borders.

8. All noisy and disorderly persons will be expelled from the grounds.

9. The Superintendent has the care of the Cemetery, and is authorized to remove all persons who violate these regulations.

10. Trespassers are liable to be fined, as provided by law.

11. Smoking is strictly prohibited in any part of the Cemetery.

12. No monumental works will be permitted to be erected in the Cemetery without a good and sufficient foundation, to be approved by the Superintendent.

N. B. Trees, shrubs and plants will be furnished to visitors by the Superintendent, at moderate charges.

---

# SUGGESTIONS TO LOT-OWNERS AND OTHERS.

The fourth clause of the deed of possession requires that the number of every lot shall be " legibly and permanently marked," at the expense of the proprietors. As those numbers can only be " permanent," that are made of iron, slate, stone or other imperishable material, proprietors whose lots are marked with *wooden* numbers are requested to substitute such indestructible material without delay, — patterns of which can be seen and ordered at the Cemetery.

Lot-owners, not original purchasers, but who have received their lots by transference from former owners and whose names have not been substituted for such former owners on the records of the Cemetery, are requested to take their deeds of possession to the Secretary of the Board, in order that such substitutions may be accurately made.

It frequently occurs that messages are sent to the Cemetery requesting graves to be opened adjoining or near the graves of persons previously interred. Where graves are not designated by stones, or otherwise, it will be impossible, in process of time, to comply with the directions thus given, unless some system designating every grave be adopted. It is recommended, therefore, that every lot-owner make a drawing of his lot on a blank page of his deed, and record on it every interment with name and date. Upon the occurrence of future interments, let a transcript of this map, with the place marked where the grave is desired to be opened, be duly sent to the Cemetery. In this way every difficulty will be obviated and an interesting family record will be made and preserved for future generations.

---

## AVENUES AND WALKS.

### AVENUES.

| | | | |
|---|---|---|---|
| Auburn, | Forest, | Mount Hope, | Rock Mound, |
| Central, | Greenwood, | Mount Vernon, | Spring Vale, |
| Channing, | Grove, | Ocean, | Union, |
| Crescent, | Highland, | Oakland, | Walnut, |
| Cypress, | Lake, | Pilgrim, | Webster. |
| Elmwood, | Laurel, | Rock, | |

### WALKS.

| | | | |
|---|---|---|---|
| Burns, | Goldsmith, | Lowell. | Spenser. |
| Cary, | Heber, | Montgomery, | Sigourney, |
| Cowper, | Holmes, | Milton, | Tennyson, |
| Dana, | Irving, | Pierpont, | Whittier. |
| Evergreen, | Landon, | Rock Dell. | |
| Glen Terrace, | Longfellow, | Shakspeare, | |

## AVENUES.

Auburn leads from Central to Central.
Central leads from front gate to back gate.
Channing leads from Crescent to Auburn.
Crescent leads from Mt. Vernon to Wabash.
Cypress leads from Central to Central.
Elmwood leads from Forest to Webster.
Forest leads from Grove to Webster.
Greenwood leads from Crescent to Spring Vale.
Grove leads from Central to Webster.
Highland leads from Central to Walnut.
Lake leads from Greenwood to Greenwood.
Laurel leads from Mt. Vernon to Walnut.
Mt. Hope leads from Central to Rock Mound.
Mt. Vernon leads from front gate to Webster.
Ocean leads from Spring Vale to Spring Vale.
Oakland leads from Forest to Webster.
Pilgrim leads from Webster to Auburn.
Rock leads from Central to Webster.
Rock Mound leads from Central to Grove.
Spring Vale leads from Auburn to Central.
Union leads from Central to Walnut.
Walnut leads from front gate to Lake.
Webster leads from Central to Central.

## WALKS.

Burns leads from Spenser to Montgomery.
Cary leads from Elmwood Avenue to Webster Avenue.
Cowper leads from Montgomery to Ocean Avenue.
Dana leads from Mt. Vernon Avenue to Laurel Avenue.
Evergreen leads from Central Avenue to Rock Mound Avenue.
Glen Terrace leads from Montgomery Walk to Ocean Avenue.
Goldsmith leads from Auburn Avenue to Rock Dell Walk.
Heber leads from Pilgrim Avenue to Union Avenue.
Holmes leads from Soldiers' Monument to Crescent Avenue.
Irving leads from Pilgrim Avenue to Union Avenue.
Landon leads from Rock Mound Avenue to Central Avenue.
Longfellow leads from Central Avenue to Mt. Vernon Avenue.
Lowell leads from Elmwood Avenue to Webster Avenue.
Montgomery leads from Pilgrim Avenue to Spring Vale Avenue.
Milton leads from Auburn Avenue to Union Avenue.
Pierpont leads from Central Avenue.
Rock Dell leads from Central Avenue to Auburn Avenue.
Shakspeare leads from Webster avenue.
Sigourney leads from Highland Avenue to Channing Avenue.
Tennyson leads from Crescent Avenue to Central and Channing Avenues.
Whittier leads from Highland Avenue to Channing Avenue.

# NAMES AND OWNERS OF LOTS,

## WITH THE RESPECTIVE NUMBERS OF EACH.

[The * indicates that the lot has two owners; the † that there are three; and the ‡ four.]

| | | | |
|---|---|---|---|
| Adams, J. Gedney | 4 | Allen, Zenas | 987 |
| Arther, James P. | 55 | Allen, Orville | 1015 |
| Allen, Joseph H. | 79 | Anthes, Matthew | 1047 |
| Abbott, Ezra | 120* | Andrews, Amanda M. | 1062 |
| Alden, George | 123 | Austin, Milton | 1075 |
| Allen, Peter | 126 | Ashcroft, Sarah | 1079 |
| Atwood, Chloe | 160† | Addison, Richard | 1246 |
| Ashe, Richard | 222 | | |
| Adams, Joseph K. . | 228 | | |
| Ayer, Elizabeth W | 253 | Beals, William | 2 |
| Adams, Samuel | 254 | Barry, Charles C. | 15* |
| Allyn, Edwin | 270 | "          " | 17* |
| Appleton, John | 277 | Bosworth, Benjamin S. | 20 |
| Adams, Obadiah F. | 298* | "          " } | 22 |
| Armstrong, Benjamin | 299 | Braman, Wm. F. | |
| Allan, George W. | 328 | Brown, Gilbert C. | 24 |
| Apthorp, Robert E. | 355 | Bugbee, Esther | 26 |
| Apollonio, N. A. | 368 | Barry, Joseph E. | 27 |
| Alesworth, R. Annie | 424 | Burditt, Benjamin A. | 29 |
| Abbott, John F. | 451 | Brown, Mary E. | 32† |
| Apthorp, Charles W. | 520 | Bartlett, Theodore | 34 |
| Ashcroft, Thomas | 530 | Breed, Aaron | 52 |
| Atkins, George P. | 574 | Bird, Isaac | 54 |
| Allen, Susan M. | 581 | Burke, Thomas F. | 57* |
| Austin, Jacob K. | 584 | Blaney, Sarah A. | 89 |
| Allen, W. H. | 617 | Beal, Warren S. | 96 |
| Allen, John | 620 | Burrill, John | 100 |
| Aymer, Francis | 626 | Brewer, Mrs. E. M. | 139 |
| Aston, James S. | 634 | Byron, Joseph C. | 144 |
| Abbott, Horace P. | 658 | Bissell, Thomas | 146 |
| Abbott, Mary W. | 762 | Brown, Horace W. | 150 |
| Adams, Nathaniel | 805 | Brownbill, John | 157 |
| Army and Navy Lot | 828 | Brooks, Kendall | 159 |
| Adams, Edward H. | 870 | Blackman, Wm. M. } | 161 |
| Austin, Samuel | 891 | Burbank, Abijah F. | |
| Abbott, Nathan F. | 909 | Barnard, Sylvester | 165 |
| Aiken, Margaret | 948 | Baker, James | 171 |

# NAMES OF OWNERS OF LOTS.

## ARRANGED BY AVENUES AND WALKS, WITH THE CONSECUTIVE NUMBER OF EACH LOT.

|  |  |  |
|---|---|---|
| 1. | E. Emily Clapp, | Central Avenue. |
| 2. | William Beals, | " |
| 3. | Isaac P. Palmer, | " |
| 4. | J. Gedney Adams, | " |
| 5. | Alexander H. Lewis, | " |
| 6. | Sarah A. L. Hardinge, | " |
| 7. | { James Flood, Ezana Flood, Anne Smith, | " " " |
| 8. | Joseph Simonds, | " |
| 9- | Horace Lothrop, | " |
| 10. | G. H. Edwards, | " |
| 11. | Bethia Neat, | " |
| 12. | { Michael S. Dodd, Lyman Seavey, | " " |
| 13. | Israel S. Trafton, | " |
| 14. | { Andrew G. Smith, William H. Munroe, | " " |
| 15. | Charles C. Barry, | " |
| 16. | Richard Miller, | " |
| 17. | { Charles C. Barry, Joseph H. Eayrs, | " " |
| 18. | David S. Tarr, | " |
| 19. | Isaac and Joshua Jenkins, | " |
| 20. | E. K. Lyford and Benjamin S. Bosworth, | " |
| 21. | ———— Houghton, | " |
| 22. | { Benjamin S. Bosworth, William F. Braman, | " " |
| 23. | Joseph P. Paine, | " |
| 24. | Gilbert C. Brown, | " |
| 25. | Ira Crawford, | " |
| 26. | Esther Bugbee, | " |
| 27. | { John Daniels, Joseph E. Barry, | " " |
| 28. | William J. Neff, | " |

| | | |
|---|---|---|
| 29. | Benjamin A. Burditt, | Central Avenue. |
| 30. { | Ira Warren,<br>Silas Warren, | "<br>" |
| 31. | Charlotte Dorr, | Landon Walk. |
| 32. { | Mary Elizabeth Brown,<br>James H. Coffin,<br>A. A. Coffin, | "<br>"<br>" |
| 33. | David Thaxter, | " |
| 34. | Theodore Bartlett, | " |
| 35. | Daniel B. and John Newhall, | " |
| 36. | Calvin Hatch, | " |
| 37. | Horace Stacey, | " |
| 38. | Charles Johnson, | " |
| 39. { | John R. Mullin,<br>John Hatchman, | "<br>" |
| 40. | William A. Orcutt, | " |
| 41. | Harriet Syrames, | " |
| 42. | William F. Haynes, | " |
| 43. | William M. Wesson, | " |
| 44. | Charles M. Foss, | " |
| 45. { | Jesse R. Warner,<br>W. H. Warner, | "<br>" |
| 46. | James A. Dupee, | " |
| 47. | Samuel B. Howard, | " |
| 48. | William H. Rymes, | " |
| 49. | Susan Downes, | " |
| 50. | Nathaniel Melcher, | " |
| 51. | George W. Hunnewell, | " |
| 52. | Aaron Breed, | " |
| 53. | John Farrington, | " |
| 54. | Isaac Bird, | " |
| 55. | James P. Arthur, | " |
| 56. | Alexander Pope, | " |
| 57. { | George S. Hardwick,<br>Thomas F. Burke, | "<br>" |
| 58. | Henry Safford, | Rock Mound Avenue. |
| 59. | James G. Lovell, | " |
| 60. | Otis Clapp, | Evergreen Walk. |
| 61. { | Nathan Wheeler,<br>Joseph Smith, | Rock Mound Avenue.<br>" |
| 62. | Moses Hadley, | Evergreen Walk. |
| 63. | Josiah Gould, | Rock Mound Avenue. |
| 64. | George W. Webster, | Evergreen Walk. |
| 65. | Henry A. and Sarah A. Turner, | Rock Mound Avenue. |
| 66. { | Samuel C. Ware,<br>John Ware,<br>Ephraim G. Ware,<br>Sarah J. Ware, | Evergreen Walk.<br>"<br>"<br>" |

| | | |
|---|---|---|
| 67. | John H. Niebuhr, | Rock Mound Avenue. |
| 68. | John P. Spooner, | Evergreen Walk. |
| 69. | Mary L. Emmons, | " |
| 70. | George W. Chase, | " |
| 71. | W. P. Cummings, | " |
| 72. | John M. Schwœrer, | " |
| 73. | Charles S. Parker, | " |
| 74. | Joseph Halstrick. | " |
| 75. | John A. Sargent, | " |
| 76. | Hosea Corthell, | " |
| 77. | Patrick O'Brien, | " |
| 78. | Robert Vose. jr., | " |
| 79. | Joseph H. Allen, | " |
| 80. | Holton Olmstead, | " |
| 81. | Lot Clark, | " |
| 82. | John H. Honey. | " |
| 83. | George L. Fisher, | " |
| 84. { | Thomas Earl, | Grove Avenue. |
| | Mrs. Catharine Hughes, | " |
| 85. { | Sabin C. Norris, | Evergreen Walk. |
| | Albert F. Norris, | " |
| 86. | William B. Harding, | Grove Avenue. |
| 87. | Joseph J. and Napoleon B. Howe, | Evergreen Walk. |
| 88. | Joseph W. Howard, | Grove Avenue. |
| 89. | Sarah A. Blaney, | Evergreen Walk. |
| 90. | Joseph L. Drew, | Grove Avenue. |
| 91. | Otis Vinal. jr., | " |
| 92. | Margaret Walsh, | " |
| 93. | Patrick O'Brien, | " |
| 94. | Joseph McIntire, | " |
| 95. | Patrick O'Brien, | " |
| 96. | Warren S. Beal, | " |
| 97. | Lemon P. Harding, | " |
| 98. | Charles F. Luther, | " |
| 99. | Jacob Herrick, | " |
| 100. | John Burrill. | " |
| 101. | William Pearce, | " |
| 102. { | John H. Josselyn, | " |
| | John H. Josselyn, jr., | " |
| 103. | Caroline T. Farnsworth, | " |
| 104. | Charles Merriam, | " |
| 105. | William F. Goodwin, | " |
| 106. | Patrick O'Brien, | " |
| 107. | William F. Godwin, | " |
| 108. | Gideon Currier, | " |
| 109. | William Durant, | " |
| 110. | Silas G. Whitney, | " |
| 111. | Louis B. Schwarz, | " |
| 112. | John Tilson, | " |

| | | |
|---|---|---|
| 113. | Patrick O'Brien, | Grove Avenue. |
| 114. | William Troup, | " |
| 115. | Elizabeth Sawtelle, | " |
| 116. | { Edward Colman, | " |
| | { Horace Jenkins, | " |
| 117. | Thomas Copeland, | " |
| 118. | Jemima Emerson, | " |
| 119. | { Louis B. Schwarz, | " |
| | { F. G. Schauffler, | " |
| 120. | { Luther Lunt, | " |
| | { Ezra Abbott, | " |
| 121. | Louis B. Schwarz, | " |
| 122. | { John T. Falls, | " |
| | { John F. Smith, | " |
| 123. | George Alden, | " |
| 124. | James H. Harding, | " |
| 125. | Jesse G. and Ebenezer P. Cotting, | " |
| 126. | Peter Allen, | Evergreen Walk. |
| 127. | Albert T. Stearns, | Grove Avenue. |
| 128. | Patrick O'Brien, | " |
| 129. | Edmund W. Parkman, | " |
| | ⌜ Mary A. Gardner, | " |
| | ⎸ Aaron A. Downes, | " |
| 130. | ⎨ Sarah E. Downes, | " |
| | ⎸ Thomas L. Downes, | " |
| | ⎸ Simon E. Downes, | " |
| | ⌞ Josephine A. Downes, | " |
| 131. | John Topham, | " |
| 132. | Ephraim Nute, | " |
| 133. | { Angus Nelson, | " |
| | { David C. Simpson, | " |
| 134. | Simeon E. Downes, | " |
| 135. | John S. Luckis, | " |
| 136. | Edmund B. Vannevar, | " |
| 137. | William W. Wood, | " |
| 138. | Susan W. Loring, | " |
| 139. | E. M. Brewer (Mrs.), | " |
| 140. | Patrick O'Brien, | " |
| 141. | Heirs of Ebenezer Weld, | " |
| 142. | Sarah Richardson, | " |
| 143. | Mary Jane Hallowell, | " |
| 144. | Joseph C. Byron, | " |
| 145. | William F. Dorman, | " |
| 146. | Thomas Bissell, | " |
| 147. | George O. Townsend, | " |
| 148. | Patrick O'Brien, | " |
| 149. | George Howland, | " |
| 150. | Horace W. Brown, | Goldsmith Walk. |
| 151. | Henry Colman, | Grove Avenue. |

| | | |
|---|---|---|
| 152. | John W. Lawson, | Goldsmith Walk. |
| 153. { | Nathaniel H. Hanscom, | " |
| | Francis Ferdinand, | " |
| 154. | Luke Jewett, | " |
| 155. | John G. and Elizabeth L. Crispin, | " |
| 156. | John Eliot, | " |
| 157. | John Brownbill, | " |
| 158. { | Thomas A Thayer, | " |
| | Louis Dennis, | " |
| 159. | Kendall Brooks, | " |
| 160. { | Henry Ramsdell, Mary A. Gass, | " |
| | Chloe Atwell and L. Stone, | " |
| 161. { | William M. Blackman, | " |
| | Abijah F. Burbank, | " |
| 162. | Daniel Webster, | " |
| 163. | George W. Redding, | " |
| 164. | Daniel French, · | " |
| 165. | Sylvester Barnard, | " |
| 166. | John Kemp, | " |
| 167. | Elizabeth L. Wright, | " |
| 168. | Joseph Penn, | " |
| 169. | Nathaniel Springfield, | " |
| 170. { | Vincent Hall, | " |
| | Charles W. Rugg, | " |
| 171. | James Baker, | " |
| 172. | Hobart M. Cable, | " |
| 173. | Stephen Baker, | " |
| 174. | Almira P. Clapp, | " |
| 175. | Samuel H. Jenks, | Rock Mound Avenue. |
| 176. { | Cyrus H. Stone, | Goldsmith Walk. |
| | James R. Fillmore, | " |
| 177. | George W. Currier, | Rock Mound Avenue. |
| 178. | Nathaniel Tucker, | Aburn Avenue. |
| 179. | Henry Molineux, | Rock Mound Avenue. |
| 180. | Daniel M. Hills, | Auburn Avenue. |
| 181. | Horace B. Darling, | Rock Mound Avenue. |
| 182. | W. S. and Joel H. Hills, | Auburn Avenue. |
| 183. | Lucius H. Briggs, | Rock Mound Avenue. |
| 184. | Ebenezer A. Hill, | Auburn Avenue. |
| 185. | Aaron H. March, | Central Avenue. |
| 186. | Leonard Harris, | Auburn Avenue. |
| 187. | Levi Flint, | Central Avenue. |
| 188. | F. W. G. Redding, | Auburn Avenue. |
| 189. | Samuel C. Richards, | Central Avenue. |
| 190. | Isaac L. Kidder, | Auburn Avenue. |
| 191. | Moses T. Durrell, | Central Avenue. |
| 192. | Daniel L. Ware, | Auburn Avenue. |
| 193. | James M. Gordon, | Central Avenue. |

| | | |
|---|---|---|
| 194. | { Nathaniel Wilton, | Auburn Avenue. |
| | { Hosea Noyes, | " |
| 195. | Jesse Russell, | Central Avenue. |
| 196. | Bridge Wheat, | Auburn Avenue. |
| 197. | S. K. Mason, | Central Avenue. |
| 198. | Thomas L. Summers, | Auburn Avenue. |
| 199. | Sarah Richardson, | Rock Avenue. |
| 200. | John K. Porter, | Auburn Avenue. |
| 201. | Royal Oliver, jr., | Rock Avenue. |
| 202. | William S. Stoddard, | Goldsmith Walk. |
| 203. | Maria Munzig, | Central Avenue. |
| 204. | John Moore, | Goldsmith Walk. |
| 205. | | |
| 206. | Esther Thomas. | Central Avenue. |
| 207. | Thomas Taylor, | Rock Avenue. |
| 208. | { Rensselaer L. Palmer, | " |
| | { Isaac B. Park, | " |
| 209. | Christopher F. Townsend, | Auburn Avenue. |
| 210.. | John W. Pierce, | Goldsmith Walk. |
| 211. | Wilmot Wilson, | Auburn Avenue. |
| 212. | Zebina Horton, | Central Avenue. |
| 213. | Charles W. Titcomb, | Auburn Avenue. |
| 214. | William S. Dillaway, | Goldsmith Walk. |
| 215. | Elizur Wright, | Auburn Avenue. |
| 216. | Thomas Gogin, | Milton Walk. |
| 217. | Richard H. Wiswell, | Auburn Avenue. |
| 218. | S. Clarence Ellis, | Central Avenue. |
| 219. | Thomas Leavitt, | Auburn Avenue. |
| 220. | Jesse Hitchcock, | Central Avenue. |
| 221. | Ebenezer Foskett, | Auburn Avenue. |
| 222. | Richard Ashe, | Goldsmith Walk. |
| 223. | Mary B. Jeffers, | Auburn Avenue. |
| 224. | William Kilner, | Goldsmith Walk. |
| 225. | James H. Upham, | Auburn Avenue. |
| 226. | Isaac M. Bassett, | Central Avenue. |
| 227. | Mary S. Beck. | Montgomery Walk. |
| 228. | Joseph K. Adams, | Central Avenue. |
| 229. | { Martha M. Omen, | Auburn Avenue. |
| | { Martha C. Stoddard. | " |
| 230. | Levi Walbridge, | Central Avenue. |
| 231. | Sarah Parks, | Auburn Avenue. |
| 232. | Joseph S. Hyde, | Central Avenue. |
| 233. | Eliza J. Burbank, | Auburn Avenue. |
| 234. | Timothy B. Mehegan, | Goldsmith Walk. |
| 235. | { Christina C. Weller, | Auburn Avenue. |
| | { Rosella C. Williams, | " |
| 236. | | |
| 237. | James F. Smith, | " |
| 238. | John Tilton, | " |

| | | |
|---|---|---|
| 239. | Jeremiah Tinkham, | Mount Hope Avenue. |
| 240. | John C. J. Brown, | Landon Walk. |
| 241. | Erastus Stoddard, | " |
| 242. | Eli Fernald, | " |
| 243. | | Channing Avenue. |
| 244. | Catharine D. Farnum, | Landon Walk. |
| 245. | William L. Champney, | " |
| 246. | Nathan Brown, | " |
| 247. | Mrs. Annah Jordan, | Central Avenue. |
| 248. | Charles H. Greenwood, | Landon Walk. |
| 249. | George Dryden, | Central Avenue. |
| 250. | Harvey Wait, | Landon Walk. |
| 251. | Sarah R. French, | Central Avenue. |
| 252. | | |
| 253. | Elizabeth W. Ayer, | Auburn Avenue. |
| 254. | Samuel Adams, | Landon Walk. |
| 255. | Thomas Britten, | Auburn Avenue. |
| 256. | H. G. Gibbs, —— Fairbanks, and | Landon Walk. |
| 258. | W. F. Stetson, | |
| 257. | Dauphin C. Kendall, | Auburn Avenue. |
| 259. | James and Susan Carlisle, | " |
| | Marcus A. Latham, | " |
| 260. | David B. Hastings, | Landon Walk. |
| 261. | Charles Thompson, | Auburn Avenue. |
| 262. | Ellis Houghton, | Goldsmith Walk. |
| 263. | Joseph B. Phelps, | Channing Avenue. |
| 264. | James Houghton, | Auburn Avenue. |
| 265. | Daniel Prescott, | " |
| 266. | Benjamin F. Hebard, | • " |
| 267. | Almira N. Lewis, | " |
| 268. | William White, | " |
| 269. | Nathaniel W. and Thomas Tileston, | " |
| 270. | Edward Allyn, | " |
| 271. | Nathaniel W. and Thomas Tileston, | " |
| 272. | Betsy Piper, | " |
| 273. | Henry T. Dyer, | " |
| 274. | Stephen Seely, | " |
| 275. | Edward B. Moore, | " |
| | McLauren F. Cook, | " |
| 276. | William Park, | " |
| 277. | John Appleton, | " |
| 278. | Francis H. Gore, | " |
| | Mary A. B. Gore, | " |
| 279. | William H. Peabody, | " |
| | Charles P. Harding. | " |
| 280. | Thomas and Alexander Christian, | Crescent Avenue. |
| 281. | Jairus A. Frost, | Central Avenue. |
| 282. | John L. Cook. | " |
| 283. | Enoch Haskell, | Auburn Avenue. |

| | | |
|---|---|---|
| 8 4. | Alanson T. Readhead, | Spring Vale Avenue. |
| 285. | Ezra S. Jackson, | Pilgrim Avenue. |
| 286. | Gideon Beck, | Auburn Avenue. |
| 287. | George Hayden, | Pilgrim Avenue. |
| 288. | William W. Capen, | Auburn Avenue. |
| 289. | Elisha Ellis, | " |
| | Daniel T. Knight, | " |
| 290. | Henry Taylor, | " |
| 291. | Thomas S. Hart, | " |
| 292. | H. N. Grover, | Grove Avenue. |
| 293. | Milton Hall, | Auburn Avenue. |
| | Zedekiah Sanger, | " |
| 294. | Sarah Stimpson, | Webster Avenue. |
| 295. | Harriet Grout, | Auburn Avenue. |
| 296. | William Sanders, | Central Avenue. |
| 297. | Joseph Hankey, | " |
| 298. | Obadiah F. Adams, | " |
| | Ebenezer Murray, | " |
| 299. | Benjamin Armstrong, | " |
| 300. | Josiah Bumstead, | Auburn Avenue. |
| 301. | William Shepherd, | Central Avenue. |
| 302. | Benjamin V. French, | " |
| 303. | Joseph P. George, | " |
| 304. | Charles S., Evelina M., and | Grove Avenue. |
| | Caroline E. Bailey, | " |
| 305. | | |
| 306. | F. Lyman Winship, | Webster Avenue. |
| 307. | Elijah Harris, | Grove Avenue. |
| | J. H. Crocker, | " |
| 308. | E. Augustus Story, | Webster Avenue. |
| 309. | Robert B. Leuchars, | " |
| 310. | Henry Munroe, jr., | Grove Avenue. |
| 311. | George Viner, | " |
| 312. | William Lawrence, | Mount Hope Avenue. |
| 313. | Alvin Hayes, | Goldsmith Walk. |
| 314. | Thomas Hill, jr., | Mount Hope Avenue. |
| 315, | Charles M. Brown, | Grove Avenue. |
| 316. | Elbridge G. Cobb, | Mount Hope Avenue. |
| | Joseph F. Cobb, | " |
| 317. | Robert Miller, | Goldsmith Walk. |
| 318. | James Hayden, | Mount Hope Avenue. |
| | Sarah Boydsson, | " |
| 319. | Abbie C. Nightingale, | " |
| 320. | Michael Hayden, | " |
| 321. | Amos F. Learnard, | Grove Avenue. |
| 322. | Gilbert Cummings, | Mount Hope Avenue. |
| 323. | Horace Dupee, | Grove Avenue. |
| 324. | Daniel Frazier, | Spring Vale Avenue. |
| | Thomas D. Classen, | " |

| | | |
|---|---|---|
| 325. | John W. Estabrooks, | Grove Avenue. |
| 326. | { Daniel C. Berry, | Spring Vale Avenue. |
| | { Cynthia Stillings, | " |
| 327. | Charles F. Mayo, | Goldsmith Walk. |
| 328. | George W. Allan, | Spring Vale Avenue. |
| 329. | Richard L. Harper, | Mount Hope Avenue. |
| 330. | { Levi Philbrook, | Spring Vale Avenue. |
| | { Job H. Perkins, | " |
| 331. | Prudence Jackson, | Central Avenue. |
| 332. | { William Peck, | Spring Vale Avenue. |
| | { Edward W. Murray, | " |
| 333. | William H. Saunders, | Central Avenue. |
| 334. | Thomas S. Johnson, | Spring Vale Avenue. |
| 335. | Job F. Bailey, | Mount Hope Avenue. |
| 336. | Elbridge and Augustus Brown, | Spring Vale Avenue. |
| 337. | James Cutler, | Mount Hope Avenue. |
| 338. | Nahum Capen, | Spring Vale Avenue. |
| 339. | { Isaac M. Lord, | Central Avenue. |
| | { Harriet S. Bryer, | " |
| 340. | Joseph Dix, | Spring Vale Avenue. |
| 341. | Ruth D. Southwick, | Rock Mound Avenue. |
| 342. | John C. Hubbard, | Spring Vale Avenue. |
| 343. | Samuel Holbrook, | Rock Mound Avenue. |
| 344. | Christian Nelson, | Spring Vale Avenue. |
| 345. | Betsey Littlefield, | Rock Mound Avenue. |
| 346. | Caroline A. Deluce, | Spring Vale Avenue. |
| 347. | Jonathan Brooks, | Rock Mound Avenue. |
| 348. | Charles Packard, | Mount Hope Avenue. |
| 349. | George Ellis. | Rock Mound Avenue. |
| 350. | Elija H. Goodwin, | Mount Hope Avenue. |
| 351. | { Asa Fillebrown, | Rock Mound Avenue. |
| | { William B. Hawes, | " |
| 352. | | Spring Vale Avenue. |
| 353. | E. H. Brainard, | Glen Walk. |
| 354. | Henry R. Mailard, | Mount Hope Avenue. |
| 355. | Robert E. Apthorp, | Spring Vale Avenue. |
| 356. | Dr. William Nichols, | " |
| 357. | George Munroe, | " |
| 358. | { Albert Pierce, | " |
| | { John E. Pierce, | " |
| 359. | John M. Dearborn, | " |
| 360. | { William A. and | " |
| | { James Neilson, | " |
| 361. | Helen Orcutt. | Central Avenue. |
| 362. | Lucy Bowthorp, | Montgomery Walk. |
| 363. | James Bowdoin Bradlee, | Spring Vale Avenue. |
| 364. | John Scates, | Montgomery Walk. |
| 365. | Albert Stanwood, | Spring Vale Avenue. |
| 366. | Benjamin Clark, | Montgomery Walk. |

| | | |
|---|---|---|
| 367. | Edward Baldwin, | Spring Vale Avenue. |
| | Marcia White, | " |
| 368. | N. A. Apollonio, | Montgomery Walk. |
| 369. | Thomas Morgan, | Spring Vale Avenue. |
| 370. | Thomas Johnson, | Montgomery Walk. |
| 371. | Bradford Sumner, | Spring Vale Avenue. |
| 372. | Harriet Clapp, | Montgomery Walk. |
| 373. | Charles Haskell, | Spring Vale Avenue. |
| 374. | John and James Dunlap, | Montgomery Walk. |
| 375. | Joseph M. Marsh, | Spring Vale Avenue. |
| 376. | Lemuel Capen, | Montgomery Walk. |
| 377. | Edward Thaxter, | Glen Walk. |
| 378. | James Rice, | Ocean Avenue. |
| 379. | Benjamin W. Gilbert. | Glen Walk. |
| 380. | Mrs. Caroline P. Whitcomb, | Ocean Avenue. |
| 381. | Henry Towle. | Glen Walk. |
| | Charles A. Towle, | " |
| 382. | George Weber. | " |
| | Frederick Dorr, | " |
| 383. | Henry Pepper Roberts, | Spring Vale Avenue. |
| 384. | Port Society of the City of Boston and its vicinity, | Ocean Avenue. |
| 385. | William B. Foster. | " |
| 386. | David Marden, | Montgomery Walk. |
| 387. | John Sabine, | Ocean Avenue. |
| 388. | Elizabeth J. Rolle, | Montgomery Walk. |
| 389. | William Makepeace, jr., | Central Avenue. |
| 390. | Ezra Harlow, | Montgomery Walk. |
| 391. | Benjamin Lyon, | Cowper Walk. |
| 392. | Samuel R. Spinney, | Montgomery Walk. |
| 393. | Hubbard Winslow, | Cowper Walk. |
| 394. | James L English, | Montgomery Walk. |
| 395. | Hubbard Winslow, | Cowper Walk. |
| 396. | James N. Tolman, | Montgomery Walk. |
| 397. | Almira Wheeler, | Cowper Walk. |
| | Caroline A. Cummings, | " |
| 398. | B. T. Loring, | Montgomery Walk. |
| 399. | George C. Robinson, | Cowper Walk. |
| 400. | Augustus C. Gale, | Montgomery Walk. |
| 401. | James W. Carter, | Cowper Walk. |
| | John Carter. Jr., | " |
| 402. | Benjamin Judkins. | Montgomery Walk. |
| 403. | Benjamin L Merrill, | Cowper Walk. |
| 404. | Elizabeth Merrill, | Montgomery Walk. |
| 405. | J. F. W. Lane. | Cowper Walk. |
| 406. | Cyrus P. Gould, | Montgomery Walk. |
| 407. | Maria F. Stimpson, | Glen Walk. |
| 408. | Joseph T. Orne, | Montgomery Walk. |
| 409. | Frederic D. Huntington, | " |

| | | |
|---|---|---|
| 410. | David D. Boyden, | Montgomery Walk· |
| 411. | Epes Sargent, | " |
| 412. | Albert Stedman, | " |
| 413. | Sarah S. Whitney. | " |
| 414. | { Jacob Norris, Josiah Knowles, | " |
| | { and Nancy Gowing, | " |
| 415. | John K. Porter, | " |
| 416. | { Francis Richards, | " |
| | { Joseph Richards, | " |
| 417. | { Otis S. Pierce, | Ocean Avenue. |
| | { Thomas Erskine, | " |
| 418. | Isaac C. Trowbridge, | Montgomery Walk. |
| 419. | Charles F. Holden, | Ocean Avenue. |
| 420. | James H. Means, | Montgomery Walk. |
| 421. | David M. Simmonds, | " |
| 422. | Owen G. Peabody, | " |
| 423. | William Scott, | " |
| 424. | { R. Annie Alesworth, | " |
| | { Sarah E. Kingman, | " |
| 425. | Asa Dodge, | " |
| 426. | William M. Wise, | " |
| 427. | Edward R. Hunt, | " |
| 428. | A. J. & J. H. Bennett, | " |
| 429. | Fanny Whipple, | " |
| 430. | { Augustus Robinson, | " |
| | { James M. Hendley, | " |
| 431. | Sarah Pike, | " |
| 432. | Parish of St. Mary's Church, | Elmwood Avenue. |
| 433. | George O. Richardson, | Montgomery Walk. |
| 434. | { Clara A. Wilkins, | " |
| | { Henry A. McGlenen, | " |
| 435. | William Lutted, | " |
| 436. | Jotham and Joseph Twitchell, | " |
| 437. | Benjamin V. French, | " |
| 438. | George M. Cook, | " |
| 439. | George G. Drew, | " |
| 440. | Samuel W. Haley, | " |
| 441. | Joseph Tobey, | " |
| 442. | Orice K. Stebbins, | " |
| 443. | George Lunt, | " |
| 444. | John E. Hesseltine, | Greenwood Avenue. |
| 445. | George E. Hayden, | Montgomery Walk. |
| 446. | Stephen B. Cram, | Greenwood Avenue. |
| 447. | Lucy M. Ball, | Montgomery Walk. |
| 448. | Perry A. Sylvester, | Greenwood Avenue. |
| 449. | J. W. Stephens, | Montgomery Walk. |
| 450. | T. E. Coolidge, | Greenwood Avenue. |
| 451. | John F. Abbott, | Montgomery Walk. |
| 452. | Nahum Jones, | Greenwood Avenue. |

| | | |
|---|---|---|
| 453. | Miles Erwin, | Montgomery Walk. |
| | Samuel Roberson, | " |
| 454. | Moses C. Greene, | Greenwood Avenue. |
| 455. | Thomas J. T. Young, | Montgomery Walk. |
| 456. | David Breese, | Heber Walk. |
| | Jane Wilcox, | " |
| 457. | Adelia Williams, | Montgomery Walk. |
| 458. | Eliza A. Tirrell, | Greenwood Avenue. |
| 459. | James B. and Mary T. Wheeler, | |
| | and Abigal Wells, | " |
| 460. | James H. Conant, | " |
| 461. | Ambrose Lovis. | " |
| 462. | Charles H. Leach, | " |
| 463. | Enoch S. Dillaway, | " |
| 464. | William Rogers, | " |
| 465. | Ephraim Merriam, | " |
| 466. | Jacob Merriam, | " |
| 467. | Granville S. Seaverns, | " |
| 468. | Catharine P. Smith, | " |
| 469. | Rufus Brackett, | " |
| 470. | Emily Clapp, | " |
| 471. | Henry F. Green, | " |
| 472. | Wulf C. J. Fries, | " |
| 473. | Henry G. Terry, | " |
| 474. | Eleazer B. Witherspoon, | " |
| •475. | Ephraim Taylor, | Montgomery Walk. |
| 476. | Mrs. Pauline Canegaly, | " |
| 477. | Horace F. Farrington, | " |
| 478. | Edmund B. Vannevar, | " |
| 479. | Chapel of Good Shepard, | Channing Avenue. |
| 480. | Samuel E. Wetherbee, | " |
| 481. | William Danforth, | Greenwood Avenue. |
| 482. | Charles M. Beckler, | Channing Avenue. |
| 483. | David S. Simpson, | " |
| 484. | Elizabeth and Lydia Fuller, | Spring Vale Avenue. |
| | Margaret A. Murray, | " |
| 485. | Andrew Pratt, | Channing Avenue. |
| 486. | Gilbert Wait, | Auburn Avenue. |
| 487. | Martin L. Whitcher, | Grove Avenue. |
| 488. | Mary E. Haley, | Channing Avenue. |
| 489. | Emily R. Williams, | Montgomery Walk. |
| 490. | Thomas, Henry W., and Wm. Gill, | Rock Dell Walk. |
| 491. | John P. Powers, | Milton Walk. |
| 492. | Thomas, Henry W., and Wm. Gill, | Rock Dell Walk. |
| 493. | D. D. Slade, | " |
| 494. | John Bowdlear, | Crescent Avenue. |
| 495. | Eliza A. Brigham, | Mount Hope Avenue. |
| 496. | Louis Mason, | Rock Mound Avenue. |
| | Jephtha C. Bruce, | " |

| | | |
|---|---|---|
| 497. | | |
| 498. | Susan L. M. Frothingham, | Goldsmith Walk. |
| 499. | James Graham, | Mount Hope Avenue. |
| 500. | J. B. Stearns, | Rock Dell Walk. |
| 501. | Oliver O. Beckler, | |
| 502. | James E. Colson, | " |
| 503. | Frederick Shunk, | Webster Avenue. |
| 504. | Joseph Carew, | Rock Dell Walk. |
| 505. | William White, | Webster Avenue. |
| 506. | Stephen Wales, | Rock Dell Walk. |
| 507. | Robert Rogerson, jr., | Webster Avenue. |
| 508. | S. B. Stebbins, | Rock Dell Walk. |
| 509. | Smith Eldredge, | Webster Avenue. |
| 510. | Mary E. Wardner, | Central Avenue. |
| 511. | Calvin Haven, | Webster Avenue. |
| 512. | Alfred J. Mercer, | Central Avenue. |
| 513. | Calvin Haven, | Webster Avenue. |
| 514. | Jane Buckley, | Central Avenue. |
| 515. | | |
| 516. | Elizabeth S. Beck, | " |
| 517. | | |
| 518. | Daniel Tenney, | Rock Dell Walk. |
| 519. | William Brown, | Webster Avenue. |
| 520. | Chas. W. Apthorp, | Rock Dell Walk. |
| 521. | Edward H. Holbrook, | Webster Avenue. |
| 522. | Nathaniel Jenkins, | Mount Hope Avenue. |
| 523. | Barnabas T. Loring, | Webster Avenue. |
| 524. | Moses Chase, | Mount Hope Avenue. |
| 525. | George Mowton, | " |
| 526. | Thomas B. Wiggin, | " |
| 527. | Almon Platts, | " |
| 528. | Ivory Corson, | " |
| 529. | Woodbury Emery, | " |
| 530. | Thomas Ashcroft, | " |
| 531. | Rebecca H. Learned, | " |
| 532. | Charles E. Davis, | " |
| 533. | Nathaniel H. Calder, | " |
| 534. | Robert Bunten, | " |
| 535. | James A. Kelley, | " |
| 536. | John J. Steger, | " |
| 537. | Lewis Currier, | " |
| 538. | Daniel B. Hallett, | Mount Hope Avenue. |
| 539. | Edmund Squire, | Evergreen Walk. |
| 540. | { Henry B. Janes, | Mount Hope Avenue. |
| | { George Souther, | " |
| 541. | Printers' Lot, | " |
| 542. | Mary E. Perkins, | " |
| 543. | { Job T. Souther, | " |
| | { Edwin B. Spinney, | " |

| | | |
|---|---|---|
| 544. | David M. Oliver and Thomas H. Oliver. | Mount Hope Avenue. |
| 545. | Hilton P. Langley, | " |
| 546. | Marshall Burnett, | Channing Avenue. |
| 547. | Leonard Hall, | Mount Hope Avenue. |
| 548. | George J. Blank, | Channing Avenue. |
| 549. | Catherine Cushing, | Mount Hope Avenue. |
| 550. | William J. Foley. | Channing Avenue. |
| 551. | Elizabeth Spencer, | Mount Hope Avenue. |
| 552. | James M. Green. | Channing Avenue. |
| 553. | Samuel C. Wilkins, | Mount Hope Avenue. |
| 554. | James H. Rist, | Channing Avenue. |
| 555. | Thomas Faunce, | Auburn Avenue. |
| 556. | Thomas D. Gerrish, | " |
| 557. | Mrs. Charles Weeber, | " |
| 558. | Frederick Weibrecht, | " |
| 559. | Robert Morss, | " |
| 560. | Catherine L. Richards, | Heber Walk. |
| 561. | Samuel Wood. | " |
| 562. | Jeremiah Sanborn, | " |
| 563. | Anthony Hanson, | Auburn Avenue. |
| 564. | Richard Woodsome, | Heber Walk. |
| 565. | Jacob Kautzmann, | " |
| 566. | Robert D. Griggs, | " |
| 567. | Edward Parmenter, | " |
| 568. | Peter Ross. | " |
| 569. | Maria Merritt, | " |
| 570. | Caroline D. Waldron, | Ocean Avenue. |
| 571. | David H. Hartshorn, | " |
| 572. | Charles Biner. | " |
| 573. | John E. Hodges, | " |
| 574. | George P. Atkins, | " |
| 575. | Mary Harris, | " |
| 576. | George Brown, | " |
| 577. | William H. Merriam, | " |
| 578. | Thomas Spinney, | " |
| 579. | James Moore, | " |
| 580. | Charles T. Brigden, | " |
| 581. | Susan M. Allen, | " |
| 582. | Agnes Bridge, | " |
| 583. | James McClearn, | Heber Walk. |
| 584. | Jacob K. Austin, | " |
| 585. | Stephen Lang, | " |
| 586. | Joseph E. Bond, | " |
| 587. | Odd Fellows' Lot, | Central Avenue. |
| 588. | Emeline P. Lovell, | " |
| 589. | Anna O. Jones, | Heber Walk. |
| 590. | Samuel Ford. | Irving Walk. |
| 591. | George Ropes, jr., | " |

| | | |
|---|---|---|
| 592. | Mrs. David Jones, | Irving Walk. |
| 593. | Charles A. Bridges, | " |
| 594. | William E. Ford, | Central Avenue. |
| 595. | Emma J. Cole, | Irving Walk. |
| 596. | Francis Ballantyne, | " |
| 597. | John Buckpitt, | " |
| 598. | Catherine Barton, | " |
| 599. | Mrs. Frances Shattuck, | " |
| 600. | Erastus B. Gould, | Channing Avenue. |
| 601. | Charles O. Pratt, | Grove Avenue. |
| 602. | { George W. Moulton, <br> { James F. Moulton, | " <br> " |
| 603. | John Hickey, | " |
| 604. | Home for Aged Men, | Rock Avenue. |
| 605. | Henry Shakeshaft, | Forest Avenue. |
| 606. | David Haggerston, | Shakspeare Walk. |
| 607. | Joshua W. Richardson, | Forest Avenue. |
| 608. | Consumptives' Home Lot, | Cypress Avenue. |
| 609. | | |
| 610. | Shadrach S. Pearce, | Crescent Avenue. |
| 611. | Elizabeth Hall, | Webster Avenue. |
| 612. | Henry W. Wilson, | " |
| 613. | Augustus King, | " |
| 614. | Charles H Parsons, | " |
| 615. | John G. Shafer, | " |
| 616. | Lewis Jones, | Webster Avenue. |
| 617. | William H. Allen, | Milton Walk. |
| 618. | Mary A. H. Redding, | Crescent Avenue. |
| 619. | Francis Dugan, | Webster Avenue. |
| 620. | John Allen, | " |
| 621. | Joseph Robinson, | Grove Avenue. |
| 622. | Charles H. Thompson, | " |
| 623. | { Francis Hall, <br> { Benjamin Buckley, | Spring Vale Avenue. <br> " |
| 624. | Charles P. Harding, | Grove Avenue. |
| 625. | Israel Webber, | Oakland Avenue. |
| 626. | Francis Aymar, | " |
| 627. | Stephen M. Grant, | " |
| 628. | Lewis Jones, | Webster Avenue. |
| 629. | Home for Little Wanderers, | Cypress Avenue. |
| 630. | J. H. Graupner, | Heber Walk. |
| 631. | Andrew J. Felt, | " |
| 632. | William Fairweather, | " |
| 633. | Emily C. Christopher, | " |
| 634. | James S. Aston, | Montgomery Walk. |
| 635. | John H. Seipp, | Heber Walk. |
| 636. | Jerusha Sherman, | " |
| 637. | Elizabeth N. Richards, | " |
| 638. | George G. Spear, | " |
| 639. | Junius M. Stephens, | " |

| | | |
|---|---|---|
| 640. | Ephraim A. Whitney, | Irving Walk. |
| 641. | Marcus V. Coffin, | Heber Walk. |
| 642. | George Remick, | Irving Walk. |
| 643. | Harriet N. Woodbury, | Heber Walk. |
| 644. | Eunice S. Hutchings, | " |
| 645. | Elbridge Currier, | " |
| 646. | Freedom D. Damon, | " |
| 647. | George Beatty, | " |
| 648. | Henry H. Carr, | " |
| 649. | William Nicholson, | " |
| 650. | William Herron, | " |
| 651. | Francis Richards, | " |
| 652. | Lemuel Tompkins, | " |
| 653. | Thomas Saunders, | Irving Walk. |
| 654. | Hannah Keller, | Heber Walk. |
| 655. | . George W. Parsons, | " |
| 656. | William E Sheridan, | Channing Avenue, |
| 657. | Henrietta Daniell, | " |
| 658. | Horace P. Abbott, | Heber Walk. |
| 659. | Elizabeth Thomas, | " |
| 660. | Lydia C. Brown. | Union Avenue. |
| 661. | Charles W. Slack, | " |
| 662. | James C. Tucker, | " |
| 663. | Stacy Baxter, | " |
| 664. | Thaddeus Gould, | " |
| 665. | John Bleakie, | " |
| 666. | Oliver Whitcomb, | " |
| 667. | Albert D. Neal. | " |
| 668. | John H. Bennett, | Greenwood Avenue. |
| 669. | James Dingley, | Union Avenue. |
| 670. | Lorenzo D. Livermore, | " |
| 671. | Charlotte Kendrick, | " |
| 672. | Amasa Bailey, | Irving Walk. |
| 673. | James Underhill, | " |
| 674. | George H. Hazlewood, | " |
| 675. | Moses Jones, | " |
| 676. | Ezra C. Waterhouse, | " |
| 677. | Hiram Stearns, | " |
| 678. | Harriet Maria Weeks, | Irving Walk. |
| 679. | Mary B. Wilmarth, | " |
| 680. | Mrs. Grace Trail, | Channing Avenue. |
| 681. | William Hall, | " |
| 682. | { Catharine Learned, | " |
| | { Mrs. Mary A. Goddard, | " |
| 683. | { Willard O. Stephens, | " |
| | { Margaret Graham, | " |
| 684. | S. C. Wheeler, | " |
| 685. | Cornelius Clapp, | " |
| 686. | William Garrett, | " |
| 687. | Robert F. Gerald, | Greenwood Avenue. |

| | | |
|---|---|---|
| 688. | Alonzo D. Peck, | Union Avenue. |
| 689. | Anna M. White, | Greenwood Avenue. |
| 690. | Edwin S. Wainwright, | " |
| 691. | Mary E. Souther, | " |
| 692. | Sarah R. Daniels, | " |
| 693. | George H. Webb, | " |
| 694. | " Temporary Home for the Destitute," | " |
| 695. | Ammi Smith, | " |
| 696. | Henry Kelley, | " |
| 697. | Sophia G. Bishop, | " |
| 698. | Thomas S. Wilder, | " |
| 699. | John Hurley, | " |
| 700. | Ezra O. F. Farrar, | Oakland Avenue. |
| 701. | Erick M. Soderberg, | " |
| 702. | William Buchanan, | " |
| 703. | John F. Farrington, | " |
| 704. | Henry Whitney, | " |
| 705. | George W. Hancock, | " |
| 706. | Elizabeth Simpson, | " |
| 707. | Sarah Jane Perry, | " |
| 708. | William Lydston, jr., | " |
| 709. | James Young, | " |
| 710. | Joseph D. Ellis, | " |
| 711. | George F. Emery, | " |
| 712. | { Mrs. Eunice Gardner, in trust for heirs of Reuben Wheeler. | " " |
| 713. | Franklin Wilkins, | " |
| 714. | John S. Sumner, | " |
| 715. | George H. Bacon, | " |
| 716. | Abraham Heilbron, | " |
| 717. | Frederick P. Conant, | " |
| 718. | William S. Locke, | " |
| 719. | Abiel Gove, | " |
| 720. | Josiah Saville, | " |
| 721. | George P. Clapp, | " |
| 722. | James W. Murray, | " |
| 723. | Gilbert D. Bugbee, | " |
| 724. | Elizabeth Bowden, | " |
| 725. | George W. Leonard, | " |
| 726. | Benjamin F. Tombs, | " |
| 727. | Elisha Turner, | " |
| 728. | William Cline, | " |
| 729. | •Francis E. Hathaway, | " |
| 730. | Susan J. Rowe, | " |
| 731. | John Green, jr., | " |
| 732. | John H. Locke, | " |
| 733. | Edward Lamphier, | " |
| 734. | Daniel Darling, | " |
| 735. | Richard W. Henshaw, | " |
| 736. | Frank Green, | " |

| | | |
|---|---|---|
| 737. | Wm. C. Hichborn, | Oakland avenue. |
| 738. | John F. Kilton, | " |
| 739. | { Jane L. D. Johnson,<br>{ Sarah J: Sumner, | "<br>" |
| 740. | Henry T. Hogan, | " |
| 741. | Jacob S. Whitney, | " |
| 742. | Thomas C. Evans, | " |
| 743. | John Parish, | " |
| 744. | Louisa M. Lapham, | " |
| 745. | Mark F. Noble, | " |
| 746. | | " |
| 747. | William Miller, | " |
| 748. | Oliver L. Winship, | " |
| 749. | Robert Knott, | " |
| 750. | William A. Brewster, | " |
| 751. | Wm. H. Morse. | " |
| 752. | { Charles Blumberg and<br>{ August Eiler, | "<br>" |
| 753. | Julian O. Mason, | " |
| 754. | Edward Bryant, | " |
| 755. | { Levi Bickford and<br>{ Abigail Kennison, | "<br>" |
| 756. | John Butler, | " |
| 757. | Aaron Joy, | " |
| 758. | Robert H. Libby, | " |
| 759. | Ammi Brown, | Webster Avenue. |
| 760. | Wm. A. Swift. | Grove Avenue. |
| 761. | Mary Jane Norton, | " |
| 762. | Mary W. Abbott, | " |
| 763. | Mary W. Chandler, | " |
| 764. | William B. Stacy, | " |
| 765. | Jacob M. Farnham, | " |
| 766. | Elizabeth Swindlehurst, | " |
| 767. | Annie M. Kemp, | " |
| 768. | George W. Seaverns, | Burns Walk. |
| 769. | John D. Young, jr., | " |
| 770. | John Dean, | " |
| 771. | Eliza Shaw, | " |
| 772. | Emily Wetherbee, | Burns and Montgomery Walk. |
| 773. | Martin Russell, | Montgomery Walk. |
| 774. | Levi D. Knights, | " |
| 775. | Hugh Macdonald, | Spencer Walk. |
| 776. | Abbie H. Gilbert, | Whittier Walk. |
| 777. | Samuel J. Bird, | Spring Vale Avenue. |
| 778. | | " |
| 779. | Jacob Pfeiffer, | Central Avenue. |
| 780. | George E. Martin, | Whittier Walk. |
| 781. | Harriet F. Swett, | " |
| 782. | Martha J. Clemens, | " |

| | | |
|---|---|---|
| 783. | James Sharp, | Whittier Walk. |
| 784. | J. S. Erskine, | " |
| 785. | Page Taylor. | " |
| 786. | James L. Wilson, | " |
| 787. | Belding D. Bingham, | " |
| 788. | Willard T. Sisson, | " |
| 789. | Peter L. Hanson. | " |
| 790. | Maria T. Goodwin, | " |
| 791. | Mrs. Mary Prescott, | " |
| 792. | Julia A. Thayer, | " |
| 793. | Richard T. Lombard, | " |
| 794. | Lendall F. Tarbett, | " |
| 795. | Charles H. Mills, | " |
| 796. | Thomas Milligan, | " |
| 797. | Edwin B. Stone, | " |
| 798. | Hiram Calef, | Sigourney Walk. |
| 799. | Galen Poole, | " |
| 800. | Henry Goldie, | " |
| 801. | Mary H. Menzicoff, | " |
| 802. | Wm. H. Wyman, | " |
| 803. | Hiram Dacey, | " |
| 804. | William E. Moore, | " |
| 805. | Nathaniel Adams, | " |
| 806. | Joseph Cooper, | " |
| 807. | Howard W. Brooks, | " |
| 808. | Frances J. Merrill, | " |
| 809. | Clement Drew, | " |
| 810. | Converse F. Pratt, | Channing Avenue. |
| 811. | Ellen Wyman. | Sigourney Walk. |
| 812. | Robert Gilchrist, | Channing Avenue. |
| 813. | Daniel Lyon, | " |
| 814. | George N. and Wm. M. Parker, | " |
| 815. | Richard Lang, | " |
| 816. | Adeline Reynolds, | " |
| 817. | Jerome B. Carpenter, | " |
| 818. | Ruth Yeaton, | Channing Avenue. |
| 819. | Thomas Ramsey, | " |
| 820. | Chester A. Collins, | " |
| 821. | Lory B. Foss, | " |
| 822. | James Morse, | " |
| 823. | Dudley R. Palmer, | " |
| 824. | Margaret B. Crane, | " |
| 825. | Richard H. Yarrington, | Union Avenue. |
| 826. | George H. Lane, | Cowper Walk. |
| 827. | Mary D. Whitney (Tomb), | Channing Avenue. |
| 828. | Army and Navy Lot, | Greenwood Avenue. |
| 829. | House of the Good Samaritan, | Webster Avenue. |
| 830. | Charles W. Simmons, | Central Avenue. |
| 831. | | " |

| | | |
|---|---|---|
| 832. | | Central Avenue. |
| 833. | | " |
| 834. | William Jennings, | " |
| 835. | | " |
| 836. | | " |
| 837. | | " |
| 838. | | " |
| 839. | | " |
| 840. | | " |
| 841. | | " |
| 842. | | " |
| 843. | | " |
| 844. | | " |
| 845. | | " |
| 846. | | " |
| 847. | | " |
| 848. | | " |
| 849. | | " |
| 850. | | " |
| 851. | | " |
| 852. | | " |
| 853. | | " |
| 854. | | " |
| 855. | | " |
| 856. | | " |
| 857. | | " |
| 858. | | " |
| 859. | William F. O. Federhen, | " |
| 860. | | " |
| 861. | Edson Newell, | " |
| 862. | | " |
| 863. | Alvah H. Peters, | " |
| 864. | | " |
| 865. | Luther Pierce, | " |
| 866. | Charles F. Thayer, | Central Avenue. |
| 867. | Horatio N. Geldert, | " |
| 868. | James H. Beck, | " |
| 869. | Willard Onion, | " |
| 870. | Edward H. Adams, | " |
| 871. | George H. Butler, | " |
| 872. | Henry A. Schoppe, . | " |
| 873. | Manley O. Butler, | " |
| 874. | James A. Wallace, | " |
| 875. | Mary A. Mellow, | Crescent Avenue. |
| 876. | Adele M. Keeler, | Central Avenue. |
| 877. | William H. Hoyt, | Elmwood Avenue. |
| 878. | Henry C. Stratton, | Central Avenue. |
| 879. | { Solomon Kenyon, Thomas F. Shuman, | Crescent Avenue. " |

| | | |
|---|---|---|
| 880. | Eunice Smith, | Central Avenue. |
| 881. | Magnus Ventress, | Crescent Avenue. |
| 882. | Martin F. Brigham, | Central Avenue. |
| 883. | Daniel B. Daly, | Crescent Avenue. |
| 884. | Daniel W. Phipps, | Central Avenue. |
| 885. | James C. Foster, 2d, | Crescent Avenue. |
| 866. | Alexander Mitchell, | Central Avenue. |
| 887. | Albert J. Bamford, | Crescent Avenue. |
| 888. | Charles H. Ellis, | Central Avenue. |
| 889. | William H. Brown, | Crescent Avenue. |
| 890. | Benjamin Rae, | Central Avenue. |
| 891. | Samuel Austin, | Crescent Avenue. |
| 892. | Oliver H. Spurr, | Central Avenue. |
| 893. | William J. Stuart, | Crescent Avenue. |
| 894. | James B. Weeks, | Central Avenue. |
| 895. | Charles F. West, | Crescent Avenue. |
| 896. | Boston Childrens' Friend Society, | Elmwood Avenue. |
| 897. | Joseph H. Wood, | Crescent Avenue. |
| 898. | Francis C. Loring, | Longfellow Walk. |
| 899. | William P. Perkins, | " |
| 900. | Betsey B. Perkins, | " |
| 901. | Harriet M. Haskell, | Milton Walk. |
| 902. | Charles C. Hood, | " |
| 803. | John B. Locke, | " |
| 904. | Wm. C. Nicholson, | " |
| 905. | Elmore F. Brackett, | " |
| 906. | Isaiah Josselyn, | " |
| 907. | Spencer Nolen, | " |
| 908. | Charles B. Townsend, | " |
| 909. | Nathan F. Abbott, | " |
| 910. | Henry Weltch, | " . |
| 911. | Mary A. Hobart, | " |
| 912. | Harriet R. Baldwin, | " |
| 913. | Benjamin B. Frederick, | Milton Walk. |
| 914. | Charles C. Priest, | " |
| 915. | Alson F. Poole, | " |
| 916. | David C. Percival, jr., | Evergreen Walk. |
| 917. | Harriet A. Betcher, | " |
| 918. | Winslow B. Lucas, | " |
| 919. | George W. Stearns, | " |
| 920. | Asa Weston, | " |
| 921. | Augustine D. Ham, | " |
| 922. | Fidelia Hawley, | " |
| 923. | John King, | " |
| 924. | Theodore D. Weld, | " |
| 925. | David H. McKay, | " |
| 926. | Edward S. Hathaway, | " |
| 927. | Resture B. Haskell, | " |
| 928. | Martha Wheeler, | " |

| | | |
|---|---|---|
| 929. | John Hawkins, | Evergreen Walk. |
| 930. | Henry F. Cooledge, | " |
| 931. | John C. Mullaly, | " |
| 932. | Samuel H. Newman, | " |
| 933. | Ferdinand Von Olker, | " |
| 934. | Charles B. Hamblen, | " |
| 935. | Elizabeth B. Pierce, | " |
| 936. | | " |
| 937. | Allen F. Eastman, | " |
| 938. | Edward C. Wilsdon, | " |
| 939. | Mary Rogers. | " |
| 940. | Albert S. Blood, | " |
| 941. | Leopold Speidel, | " |
| 942. | Henry H. Kelly, | " |
| 943. | Charles Devins, | " |
| 944. | Abbie J. Harper, | " |
| 945. | Catherine M. Plaisted, | " |
| 946. | Thomas O'Brien, | " |
| 947. | William A. Mallard, | Glen Terrace. |
| 948. | Margaret Aiken, | Evergreen Walk. |
| 949. | Eliza J. Sweetland, | Glen Terrace. |
| 950. | Thomas C. Holmes, | Evergreen Walk. |
| 951. | Charles A. Pope, | Glen Terrace. |
| 952. | David Cobb, | Evergreen Walk. |
| 953. | George H. Mears, | Glen Terrace. |
| 954. | Alonzo Johnson, | Evergreen Walk. |
| 955. | Archibald Starkweather, | Glen Terrace. |
| 956. | Elisha Stone, | Shakespeare Walk. |
| 957. | George C. Fernald, | Glen Terrace. |
| 958. | Archibald Johnston, | Central Avenue. |
| 959. | William Lovell, | Glen Terrace. |
| 960. | | " |
| 961. | Solomon and Sophia Hutchings, | Glen Terrace. |
| 962. | Mary L. Seavey, | Greenwood Avenue. |
| 963. | Robert Emerson, | " |
| 964. | Alexander C. Studley, | " |
| 965. | Jerry Hubbard, | " |
| 966. | Matthew L. Paul, | " |
| 967. | Emma K. Roberts, | " |
| 968. | Sarah M. Davenport, | " |
| 969. | Charles Wagner, | " |
| 970. | Virginia Howland, | " |
| 971. | Charles J. Hayden, | " |
| 972. | Nathan A. Bishop, | Channing Avenue. |
| 973. | Henrietta Schultz, | " |
| 974. | Catherine Gerlach, | " |
| 975. | Henry C. Smith, | " |
| 976. | George Emerson, 2d, | " |
| 977. | Martha C. Miller, | " |

| 978. | Herman Gross, | Channing Avenue. |
| 979. | Charles A. T. Bloom, | " |
| 980. | John L. Fayne, | " |
| 981. | Levi W. Johnson, | " |
| 982. | Joseph T. Whitehouse, | " |
| 983. | Lydia M. Baldwin, | " |
| 984. | Jane R. Goodnow, | " |
| 985. | Charles B. Gould, | " |
| 986. | Albert D. Swan, | " |
| 987. | Zenas Allen, | Holmes Walk. |
| 988. | Thomas Kyle, | " |
| 989. | Joseph Chandler, | " |
| 990. | { Sarah A. E. Moore, | " |
|      | { Thomas E. Wills, | " |
| 991. | Lucretia R. Littlefield, | " |
| 992. | Henry M. Goodwin, | " |
| 993. | Edward Stern, | " |
| 994. | Frederick A. W. Gay, | " |
| 995. | John Grant, | " |
| 996. | George Revere, | " |
| 997. | Ann S. Durgin, | " |
| 998. | Augustus Fuller, | " |
| 999. | Jane S. Macullar, | " |
| 1000. | Timothy Buckley, | " |
| 1001. | John A. Lewis, | " |
| 1002. | Samuel N. Piper, | " |
| 1003. | John F. Neill, | " |
| 1004. | Sarah E. Batchelder, | " |
| 1005. | Wm. S. Weitz, | " |
| 1006. | Mark Chase, | " |
| 1007. | Charles E. Wise, | " |
| 1008. | Francis W. Barton, | Holmes Walk. |
| 1009. | Mary A. Fry, | " |
| 1010. | Isaac W. Newton, | " |
| 1011. | Augustus Denton, | Longfellow Walk. |
| 1012. | City Hospital, | Central Avenue. |
| 1013. | Joseph W. Lawrence, | Greenwood Avenue. |
| 1014. | Sarah W. Hart, | " |
| 1015. | Orville Allen, | " |
| 1016. | | " |
| 1017. | Frederick O. Clark, | " |
| 1018. | John S. Welch, | " |
| 1019. | { Morris B, Rowe, | " |
|       | { Calvin A. Rowe, | " |
| 1020. | { Loammi B. Lakin, | " |
|       | { James R. Fillebrown. | " |
|       | { Samuel F. Kittredge, | " |
| 1021. | Frederick W. Dickinson, | " |
| 1022. | Harriet E. Chapman, | " |

| | | |
|---|---|---|
| 1023. | Albert French, | Greenwood Avenue. |
| 1024. | Lydia N. Merrill, | " |
| 1025. | Daniel Byron, | " |
| 1026. | Miles S. Cahill, | " |
| 1027. | John F. Berry, | " |
| 1028. | William J. Murray, | " |
| 1029. | Charles W. Sutton, | " |
| 1030. | Robert Smith, | " |
| 1031. | Alfred A. Blair, | " |
| 1032. | Eliza J. Laughton, | " |
| 1033. | Rosa Steele, | " |
| 1034. | Samuel H. Wilson, | " |
| 1035. | John Miles, | " |
| 1036. | Jane W. Howe, | " |
| 1037. | Wm. Donnely, | " |
| 1038. | David Smith, | " |
| 1039. | Joseph P. Dexter, | " |
| 1040. | Richard J. Fennelly, | " |
| 1041. | Thomas H. Childs, | Crescent Avenue. |
| 1042. | George R. Williams, | " |
| 1043. | | " |
| 1044. | Lucy M. Reed, | " |
| 1045. | Nancy Bird, | " |
| 1046. | | " |
| 1047. | Matthew Anthes, | " |
| 1048. | Warren W. Hilton, | Longfellow Walk. |
| 1049. | John S. Baker, | " |
| 1050. | Samuel D. Batchelder, | " |
| 1051. | Sarah Wellman, | " |
| 1052. | { William C. Webber, } { James Webber, } | " " |
| 1053. | Susan E. Hughes, | " |
| 1054. | James M. Stevens, | Central Avenue. |
| 1055. | Susan M. Norton, | " |
| 1056. | Serena L. Sheffield, | " |
| 1057. | Geo. F. Emery, trustee for heirs of Snelling Howell, | " |
| 1058. | Edwin Cass, | " |
| 1059. | Hannah Anderson, | " |
| 1060. | George W. Farwell, | " |
| 1061. | Robert Provan, | Tennyson Walk. |
| 1062. | Amanda M. Andrews, | " |
| 1063. | George W. Tuckerman, | " |
| 1064. | Harry C. Bonnell, | " |
| 1065. | Emerson Noyes, | " |
| 1066. | Frank Scott, | " |
| 1067. | David Donald, | " |
| 1068. | Edmund T. Smith, | " |
| 1069. | | " |

| | | |
|---|---|---|
| 1070. | | Tennyson Walk. |
| 1071. | { Alfred F. Chapman, | " |
| | { James Hastings, | " |
| 1072. | | " |
| 1073. | William B. Hilton, | " |
| 1074. | Mrs. Caroline M. Page, | " |
| 1075. | Milton Austin, | " |
| 1076. | Seneca P. Morse, | " |
| 1077. | George H. Hayden, | " |
| 1078. | S. Chapin Smith, | " |
| 1079. | { Sewall Putney and | " |
| | { Sarah Ashcroft, | " |
| 1080. | Howard Houghton, | " |
| 1081. | Edmund D. Barbour, | Channing Avenue. |
| 1082. | Levi Doolittle, | " |
| 1083. | John R. Wilson, | " |
| 1084. | John McConachy, | " |
| 1085. | Hubbard Brigham, | " |
| 1086. | E. Daniel Downes, | " |
| 1087. | Margaret B. Howard, | " |
| 1088. | Sarah Foley, | " |
| 1089. | Joel C. Warner, | " |
| 1090. | Thomas Chase, | " |
| 1091. | { James O. Evans, | " |
| | { Thomas H. Evans, jr., | " |
| 1092. | | " |
| 1093. | | " |
| 1094. | Caleb Sanderson, | Pierpont Walk. |
| 1095. | | " |
| 1096. | | " |
| 1097. | Elizabeth Hurst, | Lowell Walk. |
| 1098. | Henry K. Barnes, | " |
| 1099. | Andrew Karcher, | " |
| 1100. | Charles R. Smith, | Lowell Walk. |
| 1101. | Sarah Winchester, | " |
| 1102. | Eliza Ewer, | " |
| 1103. | John Robertson, | " |
| 1104. | | " |
| 1105. | G. A. R. Post 7, | Forest Avenue. |
| 1106. | | Lowell Walk. |
| 1107. | Burton G. Walton, | " |
| 1108. | | " |
| 1109. | | " |
| 1110. | | " |
| 1111. | | " |
| 1112. | | " |
| 1113. | | " |
| 1114. | | " |
| 1115. | Leonard Day, | " |

| | | |
|---|---|---|
| 1116. | Winfield S. Lawrence, | Lowell Walk. |
| 1117. | | " |
| 1118. | | Carey Walk. |
| 1119. | | " |
| 1120. | | " |
| 1121. | | " |
| 1122. | | " |
| 1123. | | " |
| 1124. | | " |
| 1125. | | " |
| 1126. | | " |
| 1127. | | " |
| 1128. | | " |
| 1129. | | " |
| 1130. | | " |
| 1131. | | " |
| 1132. | Henry A. Rich, | Greenwood Avenue. |
| 1133. | Sarah M. Sanders, | " |
| 1134. | Nancy H. Nichols, | " |
| 1135. | Emma A. Rogers, | " |
| 1136. | Francis H. Ward, | " |
| 1137. | Jane Burke, | " |
| 1138. | John C. Gowen, | " |
| 1139. | John Robinson. | " |
| 1140. | Caroline W. Wyman, | " |
| 1141. | Mary R. Hanaford, | " |
| 1142. | Andrew G. Smith, | " |
| 1143. | | Crescent Avenue. |
| 1144. | | " |
| 1145. | | Greenwood Avenue. |
| 1146. | | |
| 1147. | | |
| 1148. | | |
| 1149. | | |
| 1150. | | |
| 1151. | | |
| 1152. | | |
| 1153. | | |
| 1154. | | |
| 1155. | | |
| 1156. | | |
| 1157. | George G. Brown, | Crescent Avenue. |
| 1158. | | |
| 1159. | Henry Morrison, | " |
| 1160. | John C. Loud, | " |
| 1161. | | |
| 1162. | Frederick N. Tirrell, | " |
| 1163. | | |
| 1164. | Denton G. Woodvine, | " |

1165.
1166.
1167.
1168.
1169.
1170.
1171.
1172.
1173.
1174.
1175.
1176.
1177.
1178.
1179. John Sharland, Central Avenue.
1180. John Taylor, "
1181.
1182. Alonzo W. Folsom, "
1183. Harriet S. and Frederick Coombes, "
1184.
1185. Ann Smart, "
1186.
1187.
1188. Laura J. Brown, Tennyson Walk.
1189.
1190.
1191.
1192.
1193.
1194.
1195.
1196. Orson D. Newhall, "
1197.
1198.
1199. Eliza A. Blodgett, "
1200.
1201.
1202.
1203.
1204.
1205. John L. Geddes, "
1206.
1207. Eliza F. Palmer, "
1208.
1209. Sarah A. Utley, "
1210.
1211.
1212.
1213.

| | | |
|---|---|---|
| 1214. | | |
| 1215. | | |
| 1216. | | |
| 1217. | | |
| 1218. | | |
| 1219. | | |
| 1220. | | |
| 1221. | | |
| 1222. | | |
| 1223. | | |
| 1224. | | |
| 1225. | Emily Wilcox, | Tennyson Walk. |
| 1226. | | |
| 1227. | Sidney A. Stetson, | Channing Avenue. |
| 1228. | | |
| 1229. | | |
| 1230. | | |
| 1231. | | |
| 1232. | | |
| 1233. | John Elliott, | " |
| 1234. | | |
| 1235. | | |
| 1236. | | |
| 1237. | | |
| 1238. | | |
| 1239. | | |
| 1240. | | |
| 1241. | | |
| 1242. | | |
| 1243. | Francis E. Hathaway, | " |
| 1244. | Charles S. Parker, | " |
| 1245. | John W. Gleason, | " |
| 1246. | Richard Addison, | " |

www.ingramcontent.com/pod-product-compliance
Lightning Source LLC
Chambersburg PA
CBHW021635270326
41931CB00008B/1042